Brain-Teasers

BOOK TWO

THEY WILL DRIVE YOU CRAZY!

Brown Watson
ENGLAND

THE BIRDS

How many birds are there in each tree?

• There are 30 birds in total.
• There is more than one bird in each tree.
• There is a different number of birds in each tree.
• The total number of birds in the two smaller trees is less than half a dozen.
• The smallest tree does not have the least number of birds.
• The biggest tree has three times more birds than the tree in the middle.
• The tree with a hole in the trunk has as many birds as all three trees to the left of it.

CAN-CAN!

In each row there is a can which does not have a number. Can you work out what the missing numbers should be?

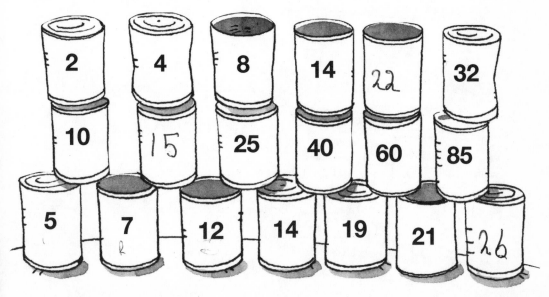

2	4	8	14	22	32
10	15	25	40	60	85
5	7	12	14	19	21	26

MALE AND FEMALE

Draw a line to join up each female animal with each male.

ewe	bull
goose	boar
sow	buck
cow	billy
doe	gander
nanny	ram

WORD SEARCH

In this word search puzzle there are six vegetables and six fruits to find. The words go across and down.

C	C	A	R	R	O	T	M
P	E	A	S	C	R	U	E
E	G	B	P	E	A	R	G
A	O	N	I	O	N	A	G
C	A	B	B	A	G	E	R
H	P	B	A	S	E	A	A
A	P	A	R	S	N	I	P
S	L	E	T	T	U	C	E
M	E	L	O	N	M	C	S

SPOT SEVEN DIFFERENCES

Can you find seven ways in which these two drawings are different?

THE SAILING SHIPS

Can you decide which
should be the ninth ship?
Is it A, B or C?

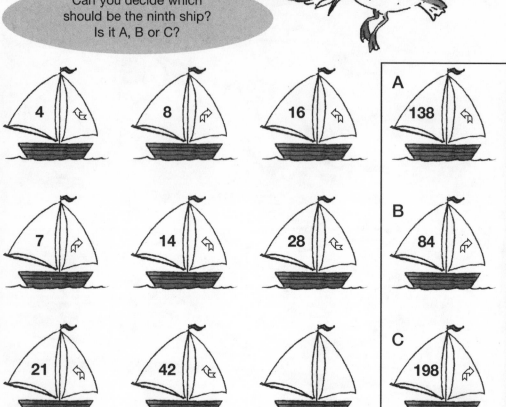

SAILORS' KNOTS

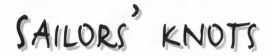

Imagine you are pulling the two ends of each rope. Three of the ropes would tie a knot. Which ones are they?

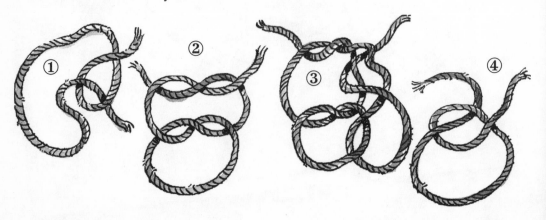

BIRTHDAY PARTY!

Mark is six today. He has invited five friends to his birthday party. At 4 o'clock they will sit down to tea. Can you decide who will sit where?

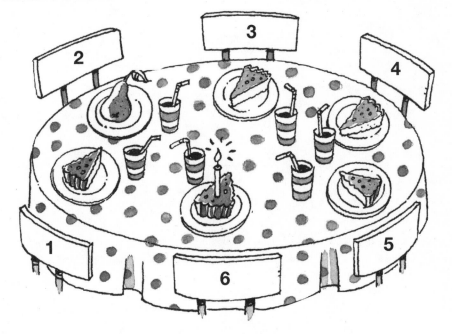

Isabel sits next to Mark.
Julie sits between two boys.
William sits facing Mark.
Marina does not eat cake.
Isabel is not facing Marina.
Thomas sits beside Mark.

Chair 1: ....
Chair 2: ....
Chair 3: ....
Chair 4: ....
Chair 5 ....
Chair 6: ......Mark...............

NAIL PROBLEM!

You can see there is a mistake in this sum! 1 minus 3 does not equal 2! But you only need to move one nail to make the sum right. How is it done?

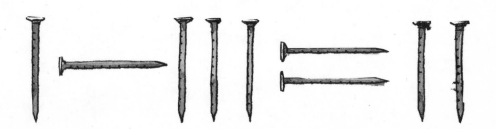

EQUAL PARTS

Can you divide this square into 4 equal parts? Make sure that each part contains 4 different creatures!

SUMS IN CODE

These sums look very odd, but you can do them by replacing each sign with a number. Of course, the sums must work out right! One clue – somewhere among the sums you will find the number 1495.

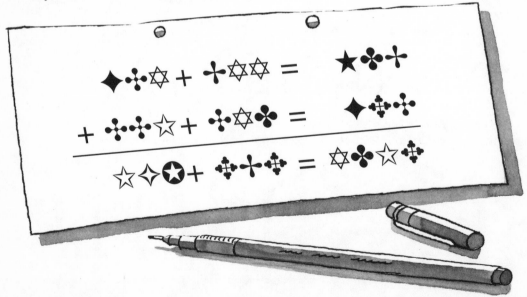

I SPY!

This grid consists of 8 rows, each with 7 symbols. Look carefully at these rows and see if you can answer the questions which follow.

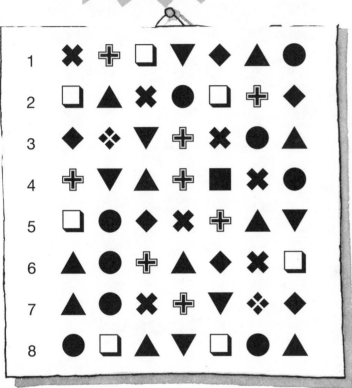

1. How many different symbols can you find? . . . .

2. Which two rows are exactly the opposite of each other? . . . .

3. Which rows contain the same symbols, but in a different order? . . . .

4. Which symbol appears the least? . . . .

5. Which symbol appears the most? . . . .

6. In which row can you find a symbol which is not seen anywhere else? . . . .

7. Is there a row which contains all the symbols? . . . .

9

CUBE PUZZLE

This big cube is made up of small cubes, but a number of small cubes are missing.

How many small cubes are needed to complete the big cube?

. . . .

How many small cubes will there be in the big cube?

. . . .

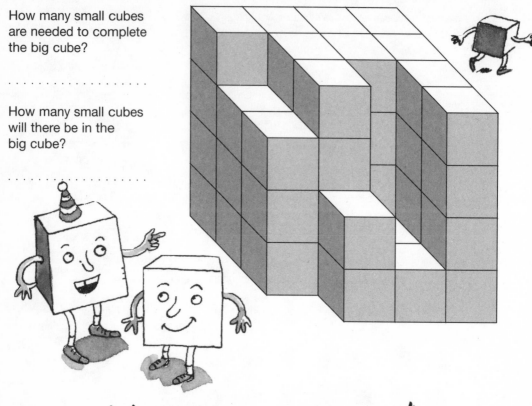

NUMBER ROBBERY!

Certain numbers and signs have been stolen from this grid. Can you put them back where they should go?

425			=	
−	■	■	−	■	−
		−	275	=	
=	■		=	■	=
32			=	14

TREASURE CHEST

This chest contains one word with eight letters! To find it, take away the number of letters in each row, across and down, as shown by the numbers. You will be left with two letters in each row across. Make sure you keep the letters that you need!

	2	2	1	3
2	D	G	E	F
2	L	C	E	I
2	M	O	B	H
2	W	E	Z	R

THE CASTLE MOAT

These castle ruins are surrounded by a moat, 5 metres wide on all sides. There is no bridge, but you have two planks, each 4 metres long, to cross the moat. How would you place these two planks so that you can cross the moat?

JOB AND PETS

For each person in this puzzle, we want to know which pet he or she owns and what job the parent does. Write the answers in the grid. Just put a plus sign (+) in the square to indicate the job or the animal for each person and write a minus sign (-) to indicate the 'wrong' job and the 'wrong' animal.

	cat	dog	canary	pony	baker	chauffeur	teacher	postman
Christopher					+	-	-	-
Ralph					-			
Anne					-			
Julia					-			

We know that:
- Christopher's dad is a baker (we have already written a + sign in the row for Christopher under the word 'baker' and a - sign in the other squares in the same row and column. We now know that the parents of the other three people are not bakers.)
- Anne does not have a cat.
- Christopher loves his dog.
- Julia's dad does not have a car.
- One of the boys has a pony.
- The chauffeur does not have any sons.
- Julia is not the daughter of a teacher.
- Julia's cat is black.
- The postman has a daughter.

A CUCUMBER AND A HALF!

A cucumber weighs 150 grams more
than a half cucumber.
How much do one and
a half cucumbers weigh?

VEHICLES

In this puzzle, each vehicle has been given a secret number from 1 to 5.

What is the value of each vehicle?

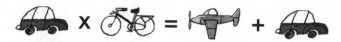

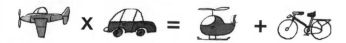

 =

 =

 =

 =

 =

ON THE FARM

The farmer wants to divide his field into 4 equal parts. In each part he needs to have one horse, one cow, one sheep, one pig and one hen. Can you help him?

THE MYSTICAL MAZE

Can you find the way out of this maze?

THE MATCHSTICK FISH

At present, the matchstick fish is swimming to the left. Can you make it swim to the right, by moving just 3 matchsticks?

FLOWER POWER

On this piece of material each flower is equal to a number. The total of the numbers in each row (across and down) is shown on the pin cushion. Find the number for each flower and write it on the ruler.

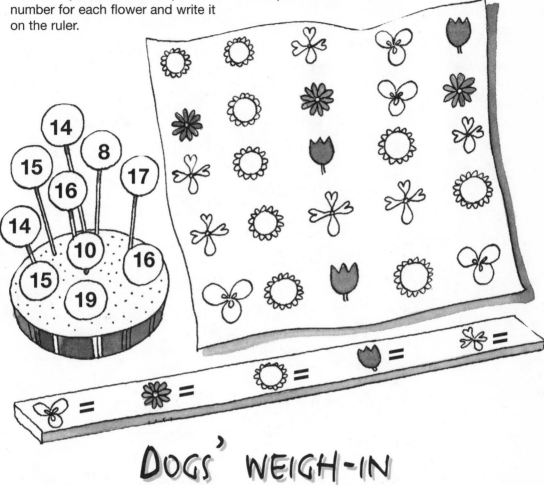

DOGS' WEIGH-IN

The kennels where Barker is staying has different breeds of dogs boarding there. Three of these breeds weighed in today and here is the result:
Each Yorkshire Terrier weighs 3 kilos.
Each Pekingnese weighs 5 kilos.
Each Poodle weighs 8 kilos.

The total weight of all the dogs put together is 22 kilos. So how many dogs of each breed are there?

THE MAGIC CARPET

Here are three sections of pattern. Can you find them in the magic carpet?

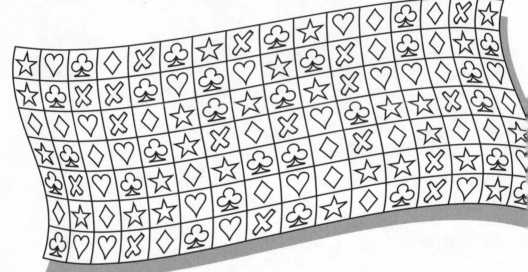

PYRAMID PUZZLE

Who is buried inside the pyramid?

The mother of the person who is inside the pyramid was the mother-in-law of my mother.

SEA BATTLE

The 10 ships alongside the grid (which is the sea) must be placed inside. The ships must not touch each other. To the left of each row and at the top of each column, a number indicates the number of squares which can be filled by a section of the ship in this row or column. To help you, some squares have already been filled in.
One tip: write the minus sign (-) in the squares which cannot be filled in. We have already done this in some of the sections.

FOLLOW ON!

Each row of numbers forms a series.
What are the last numbers in each row?

a. 4 8 10 20 22 44 46 ? ?

b. 5 6 8 11 15 ? ?

c. 1 1 2 6 24 ? ?

THE TREE

Once you have written the words in this crossword puzzle, you will find the name of a tree beneath the arrow.

1. Opposite of healthy.
2. A bird which can talk.
3. Tiny piece of bread or cake.
4. Not short!
5. Month after April.
6. Seat without a back.
7. A baby's toy.
8. A wonderful meal.

VISITING CARDS

Four people have dropped their visiting cards. Can you rearrange the letters of their names to discover which job each one does?

JAN LISTOUR

ART CETICH

STAN TARROL

IAN CISUM

THE MATCHSTICK HOUSE

The front of this house is facing left. Can you make it face right, by moving just 2 matchsticks?

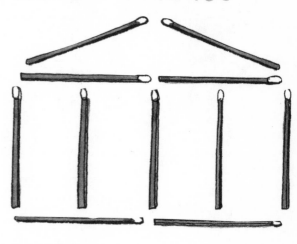

THE MATCHSTICK PALACE

This palace is built from 11 matchsticks. Can you make 11 squares by moving 4 matchsticks?

THE CLOCK

At exactly 6 o'clock, Aunt Flora moves the little hand on the clock to the place where the big hand was, and the big hand to the place where the little hand was. What time will it be then?

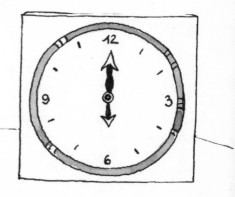

HOLIDAYS

Four people are spending
their holidays abroad.
1) Where is each one going?
2) At what time of year?
3) Where will they be staying?

	Luxembourg	Norway	Spain	Italy	1-15 July	20-31 July	1-15 August	1-31 August	Tent	With an aunt	Flat	Hotel
Jeremy		–										
Emma	–	+	–	–						–	–	
Annette		–										
Tom		–										

Fill in the right squares with a plus (+) sign, and the squares which do NOT apply with a minus (-) sign. The facts are:-

• Emma goes to Norway in July (we have already filled in the right squares for you).
• The two boys are going to southern Europe.
• Tom does not have an aunt.
• Jeremy will be away on holiday the longest.
• Tom is going with his friend to a campsite.
• Annette is renting a flat for the first fortnight in July.
• The aunt lives in Spain.
• Tom is going to Italy, but not staying in a hotel.

THE SHIP GRID

Each number inside the anchor chain has a place on this grid!

18 - 19 - 22 - 37 - 39 - 40 - 42
- 46 - 50 - 53 - 57 - 72 - 83 - 84 - 98

126 - 189 - 201 - 279 - 356 - 361 - 399 - 456
478 - 561 - 628 - 655 - 785 - 820 - 829 - 898

1234 - 3245 - 4210 - 4970 - 6005 - 6581

36108 - 45428

187605 - 416723

THE DOWNPOUR

Yesterday, Mr. Dent went out in the rain. He had neither a hat, nor an umbrella. His clothes were soaked, yet not one hair on his head was even damp. Can you guess why?

FAIR SHARES

How can you cut this cake into 8 equal pieces, by making only 3 cuts?

PEELING APPLES

Giles, David, Ann, Emily and Bruno have peeled lots of apples.
Each has a bucket with their name on it.
How many apples are there in each bucket?

- Between them, the 5 children have peeled 25 apples.
- There is a different number of apples in each bucket.
- In the biggest bucket there is the least number of apples, but more than one apple.
- The smallest bucket contains half a dozen apples.
- The bucket in the centre contains as many apples as the two buckets on either side of it, but still less than ten.
- Bruno's bucket contains three apples more than the biggest bucket.

MATCHSTICK PUZZLE

Can you make 3 triangles by taking away 3 matchsticks?

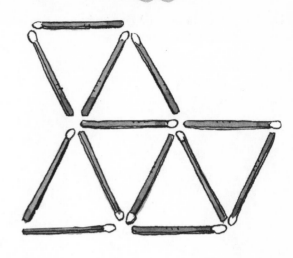

IMPOSSIBLE!

There are three mistakes in this drawing. Look hard and think carefully! Can you see what they are?

THE CUBE QUESTION

This big cube is made up of a number of smaller cubes. You can see that there are some missing. How many?

SHEEP IN THE MEADOW

Farmer Jones likes keeping sheep! He takes them into a square-shaped meadow with a tree at each corner. The farmer wants to get more sheep, so he needs to make the meadow larger. However, he wants to keep the meadow square, and to keep the 4 trees where they are. Can you help him?

THE STORYTELLERS

Which is which?

We know that:
- Gerald never tells lies.
- Charles tells lies sometimes.
- Dennis tells lies all the time.

1 = ...

2 = ...

3 = ...

NUMBER GRIDS

Complete these grids by filling in the missing numbers and signs.

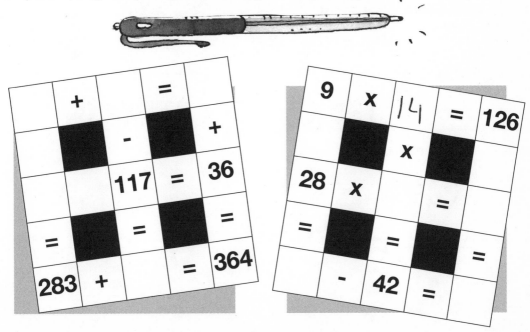

25

ANIMAL NUMBERS

Each animal always represents the same number.
Only the numbers 6 and 7 are not represented by an animal.
One clue: the numbers 8 and 9 are not used.
Can you solve the puzzle by filling in the number each animal represents?

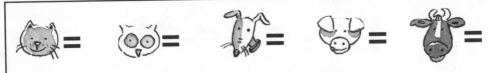

A SERIES OF LETTERS

What is the last letter in each row?

26

THE BAR

Five people, A, B, C, D and E, are sitting in a bar. Each one has a glass, illustrated by a little circle. Who are the people and what are they drinking?

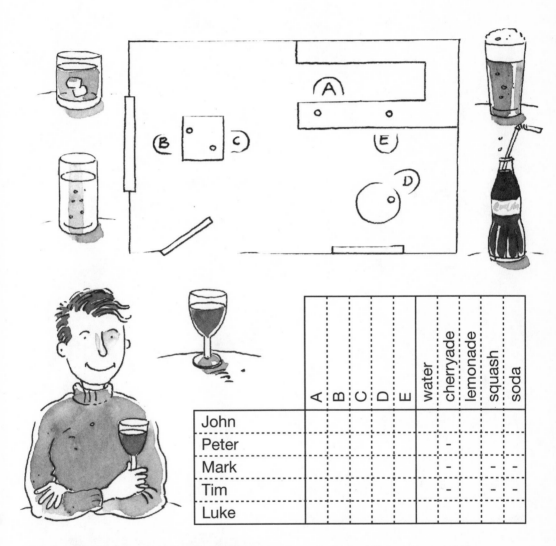

	A	B	C	D	E	water	cherryade	lemonade	squash	soda
John										
Peter							-			
Mark							-		-	-
Tim							-		-	-
Luke										

- Mark and Tim never drink cherryade, squash or soda and Peter does not like cherryade. (We have already filled in the right squares).
- The man at the bar is called Mark. He drinks lemonade.
- John and Tim are playing cards together. Tim does not have his back to the window.
- The person sitting at the round table is drinking soda.
- Mark speaks to Luke, who has just come in.
- John does not drink soda.
- There is a glass of cherryade on the bar.

27

THE TWIN CLOWNS

Two of these clowns are exactly the same. Can you find them?

TWINS OR NOT?

Two boys were born on the same day in the same year. Both have the same mother, but they are not twins! How can this be possible?

AN AMAZING APPLE TART!

Donna's dad has made the most wonderful apple tart! The moment he puts it on the table, Donna takes a piece.
Do you know how to find the piece she has cut?

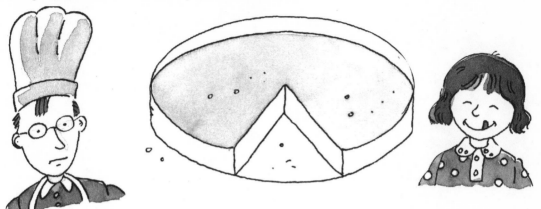

CASTLE UNDER SIEGE

The castle is besieged by the enemy! As you see from the drawing on the left, each side of the castle is occupied by 90 enemy soldiers. The number of soldiers in each group is shown on their flag.
120 enemy soldiers have been taken prisoner. No more soldiers have been brought in, yet there are still 90 enemy soldiers on each side. Can you explain this?
Show the number of enemy soldiers on each flag on the drawing to the right.

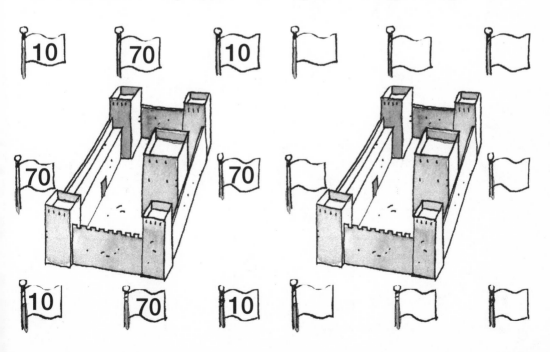

29

PYRAMID OF NUMBERS

Each stone on this pyramid should be inscribed with a number. Each of these numbers is the total of the two numbers underneath it.

THE STARRY SKY

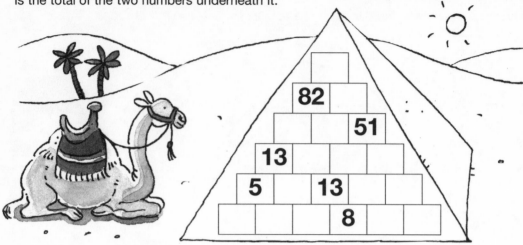

Each heavenly body and the space ship is equal to a number. The total of the numbers in each row, across and down, is shown on the right or at the bottom. Can you write the correct number for each little drawing?

NUMBERED FURNITURE

Do the following sums by working out the right number for each piece of furniture. The sum shown in the square will help you.

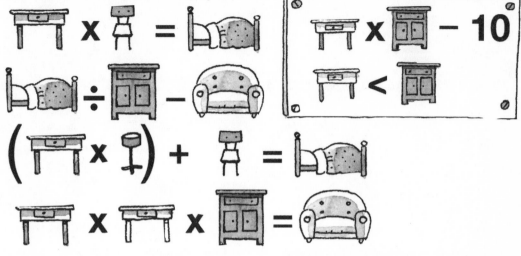

THE INTRUDER

Mary is staying in a Spanish hotel with 22 rooms.
Her room is on the top floor.
One evening, she gets ready to go for dinner with Juanita, a Spanish girl she has met.
Combing her hair in front of her bathroom mirror, she hears a knock at the door.
'That must be Juanita,' she thinks to herself.
But, in the mirror, she sees a young man coming into her room.
He looks all round, then, seeing Mary, says: 'Oh, sorry, I've come in the wrong door. I am in the next room!'
As soon as he has gone, Mary calls the hotel detective.
Soon after, the young man is stopped by the police.
He is the burglar they have been tracking for the last few weeks.

How did Mary guess that he was lying?

ON THE SEE-SAW

How many dogs would have to get on to the third see-saw to make it balance?

BARRIER PROBLEM

A farmer has 8 cows. Each one is penned separately between 4 barriers (see the drawing). One day, 3 barriers are stolen. How can the farmer arrange what is left, so that each cow is still penned inside 4 barriers?

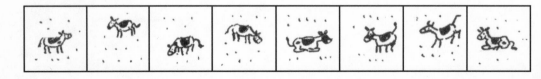

FLOWERS

John's mother has a birthday in August, when the family is on holiday in Spain. John goes to the Spanish florist shop to buy a bunch of flowers for his mother.

For 200 pesetas, John can buy 8 roses. But he wants to buy some other flowers as well. He looks at the prices and sees that 2 carnations cost as much as 1 tulip and 1 rose together.
1 rose costs 8 pesetas more than 1 tulip. At last, John buys 4 roses, 3 tulips and 2 carnations. How much does the bunch of flowers cost?

ALL AT SEA!

Each vessel represents a different number. What is the number value of each vessel?

$$\text{⛵} - \text{🚢} = \text{🛥}$$

$$(\text{🛥} + \text{🛥}) \times 2 = \text{⛵}$$

$$\text{⛵} + \text{🛥} = 100$$

$$\text{🚢} = \text{🛶} + \text{🛥}$$

$$\text{🚢} = \qquad \text{🛥} = \qquad \text{🛶} = \qquad \text{⛵} =$$

THE TILES

The roof of this house was damaged in a storm. 4 tiles are broken. Each of the broken tiles is touching 8 other tiles. Can you work out which are the broken tiles. We know that:

- each broken tile is touching at least one A and three C tiles.
- No broken tile touches an E tile.
- Each broken tile touches no more than two B tiles.

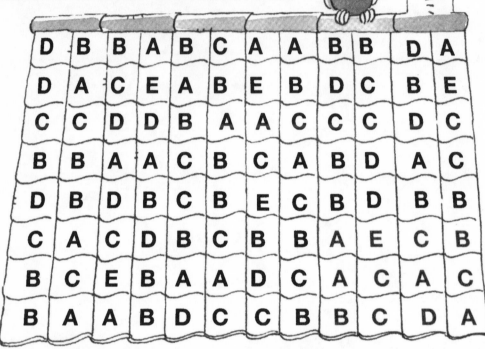

D	B	B	A	B	C	A	A	B	B	D	A
D	A	C	E	A	B	E	B	D	C	B	E
C	C	D	D	B	A	A	C	C	C	D	C
B	B	A	A	C	B	C	A	B	D	A	C
D	B	D	B	C	B	E	C	B	D	B	B
C	A	C	D	B	C	B	B	A	E	C	B
B	C	E	B	A	A	D	C	A	C	A	C
B	A	A	B	D	C	C	B	B	C	D	A

TWO BUCKETS OF WATER

You have 2 empty buckets. In one bucket, you can put exactly 5 litres of water. In the other, you can put exactly 3 litres of water. Now, you need exactly 4 litres of water.

How would you measure exactly 4 litres of water, using only the two buckets?

THE UNFINISHED PUZZLE

5 pieces are needed to finish the puzzle below. However, it seems that someone has mixed up the pieces from 2 different puzzles, because there are 8 pieces left! Can you work out which pieces belong to another puzzle?

THE LETTER-BOXES

In this picture there are 4 houses (A, B, C and D), and four letter boxes (a, b, c and d). Each owner wants to build a path linking their house with their letter box.

The paths must join A with a, B with b, C with c and D with d. Can you draw these 4 paths on the picture? The paths must neither cross each other nor cross one of the existing paths.

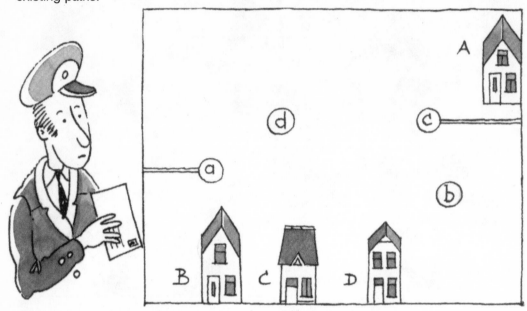

BROKEN VASE

Which broken piece will complete the vase?

AT THE MARKET

On holiday you want to buy fruit and vegetables at the market. It is so early that the stall-holder has not yet had time to mark all the prices in francs.
Can you help him?

We know that:
- 1 kg potatoes and 1 kg tomatoes together cost as much as 1 kg bananas.
- 3 kg carrots cost as much as 1 kg grapes.
- Tomatoes cost 4 times more than potatoes.
- 5 kg of grapes cost as much as 10 kg of apples.
- The total price per kilo of all the fruits (apples, pears, bananas, grapes), is three times higher than the price of the vegetables.

apples 45fr/kg

pears

bananas

carrots

potatoes

tomatoes 40fr/kg

grapes

NEWSPAPER READERS

Two fathers and two sons go to a newspaper kiosk. Each one buys a newspaper. But when they get back they have only three newspapers.
Why is this?

MIX-UP!

Can you sort out the mixed-up letters in the left-hand column to make a word? Write each one in the right-hand column. You will see the name of a flower in the column underneath the arrow.

C	E	N	D	A
S	N	E	A	B
S	T	E	A	P
T	R	E	A	L
O	C	T	U	R
S	U	N	E	R
N	A	S	T	I
S	L	I	S	A
T	R	O	U	E
T	I	M	I	L

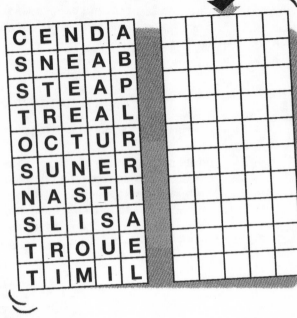

HIDDEN ANIMALS

Can you find an animal hidden in each of these sentences? Underline the animal when you find it.

1. 'I want to be a really good dancer!' said Bella.

2. The twins wanted a party.

3. You need to use a lot of paste on wallpaper.

4. The monk eyed the beggar with pity.

5. The maze branched in all directions.

6. Jean came late for the barbecue.

PERFECT BALANCE!

How many cones must be put on the fourth see-saw to make it balance?

ENJOY YOUR MEAL

What is each person eating and drinking?

	Bread	Spaghetti	Chicken	Pizza	Water	Squash	Cola	Lemonade
Claire			–					
Dawn			–					
Jack								
Matthew								

- One of the boys is eating chicken (we have already filled in the right squares).
- One of the girls is drinking squash.
- Dawn is eating a roll. She does not like squash.
- Matthew is drinking cola.
- The glass of squash goes with the plate of pasta.
- Neither of the boys is drinking water.
- Whoever is drinking lemonade is also eating chicken.

STARS IN A SQUARE

Each star must be surrounded by the numbers 1 - 8.

You must not put two of the same number around the same star!

	1		4		5	7
4	☆	3	☆	1	☆	
	8		5		2	
4	☆		☆	8	☆	5
1		7	1	4	7	
6	☆	2	☆		☆	2
	3			5	8	

THE THREE BANDITS

George, Gus and Willy are all suspected of burglary. They are questioned by a police inspector. He knows that the three suspects all tell lies. However, he also knows which one is guilty. Do you?

Gus is guilty!

I am guilty!

George is guilty!

George

Gus

WILLY

PYRAMID OF EGGS

Each egg is equal to a number. Each number is the total of the two numbers below.
Can you put the right number on each egg?

THE TWIN GRIDS

Two of these grids are exactly the same. Which ones are they?
Watch out – the grids can be turned on to any side.

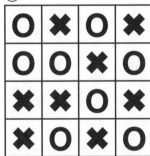

CREEPY-CRAWLIES

Each creepy-crawly has been given a number. The sum of the numbers in each row (across and down) is shown on the right or at the bottom. Can you put the right number beside each creepy-crawly?

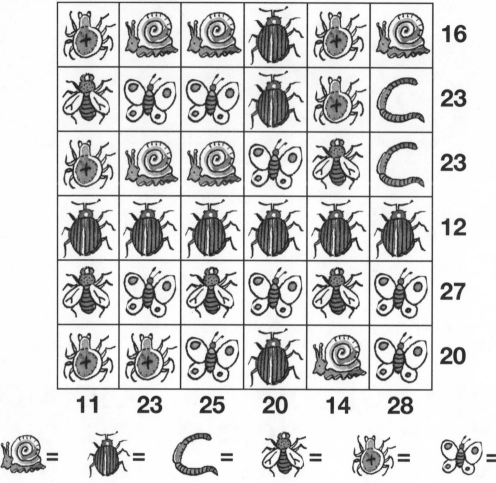

HENS AND EGGS

Five hens lay 5 eggs in 5 minutes. How long would it take 100 hens to lay 100 eggs?

THE CIRCLES

Which of the 8 circles in the box on the right belongs in the empty space?

STAR SUM

Each type of star represents a different number. One of the numbers in this sum is 1997. Can you try finishing the sum?

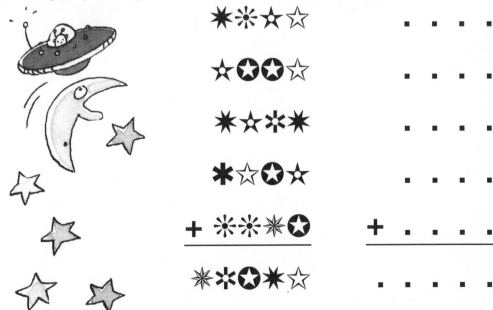

FIND THE WITNESS

The detective is searching for Eric, who is the only witness to a break-in. The detective knows Eric's address, but he is a student who shares a house with other students living on the same floor – Luke, Martin, Colin, Andrew and Mike. Can you help the detective find Eric's room? He knows that:

- Luke's room only has one door.
- To get into his room, Mike must go through the room next door.
- Martin's room is next to the toilets. This room is next to Luke's.
- Mike and Colin are neighbours, but their rooms do not have a connecting door.
- Colin's room is bigger than Mike's.
- Andrew's room and Luke's room are on the same side.
- Eric's room is not next to Luke's room.

The detective will find Eric in room ....

THE BEEHIVE

Each black honeycomb must be surrounded by the numbers 1 - 6. Just make sure that the same numbers are never next to each other!

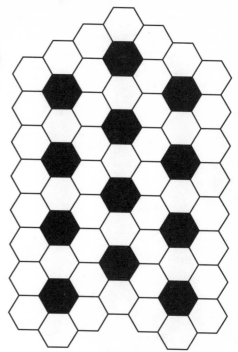

THE HIDDEN GRID

This little grid is hidden somewhere in the large grid.

Can you find it?

☹	2	☺
4	☺	6
☺	8	☹

2	6	☺	☹	2	☺	4	☹	2	☺
8	☺	4	4	☺	6	6	☺	☹	8
☺	2	☹	8	8	☹	☺	4	☺	6
☹	2	☺	☺	2	6	☹	☺	2	☺
4	☺	6	☺	☹	☹	2	☺	4	☹
☹	8	☺	6	☺	4	☺	6	☹	8
☺	2	☹	4	☹	☺	8	☹	☺	2
6	8	☺	☺	2	☺	☹	☺	☹	4
4	☺	☺	4	☺	6	☺	2	6	☺
☺	☹	2	6	8	☹	4	☹	☺	8

45

THE MAGIC SQUARE

In this magic square, the sum of each of the row of numbers (across, down and diagonally) is always the same. Complete the magic square, remembering that the numbers in each row must add up to 111.

35	1			19	24
	32	7		23	
31		2	22		20
8	28			10	15
30		34	12	14	
4	36		13		11

IN A SERIES

Finish each row by filling in all the squares with the right number or letter.

| 3 | 6 | 4 | 8 | 6 | 12 | |

| A | | I | M | Q | | Y |

| 100 | 90 | 85 | 75 | 70 | | 55 |

| Z / 128 | X / 64 | | T / 16 | R / 8 | P / 4 | |

46

CODED LETTER

Countess Marguerite Van de Fochy lives alone in her castle. One day, she decides to write a coded letter to Kiwi, her old maidservant. Each symbol represents a letter of the alphabet. Can you decode her letter?

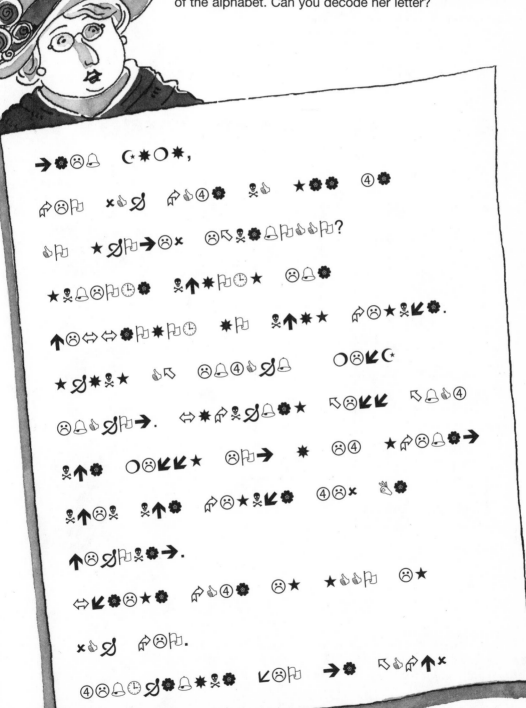

NAVAL BATTLE

The 10 ships alongside this grid must all be placed in the grid without touching each other. Beside each row a figure shows the number of squares which can be filled by parts of a ship in that row. To help you, some squares are already filled in. One tip – write the minus sign (-) in the squares which must not be filled. We have already done this in certain squares.

LIFT PROBLEM

A lady lives on the tenth floor of a building. Each morning when she goes to work she takes the lift to the ground floor. When she returns each evening, she takes the lift to the eighth floor then walks up to the tenth floor. Why doesn't she go up to the tenth floor in the lift?

COME TO THE CIRCUS

Gerald, Perry, William and John are performers in a circus.
What colour costume do they each wear?
What act do they each do?
In which town are they appearing?

	blue	yellow	red	white	clown	trapeze	artist	horse rider	Rotterdam	Cologne	Brussels	Paris
Gerald							−					
Perry							−					
William							−					
John			−		−	−	+	−				

We know that:

John does not have a red costume. He works with animals. (We have already filled in the right squares for this information.)
• Peter makes people cry with laughter in Brussels.
• You could see William working in Rotterdam.
• The horse rider has a blue costume. He is not in Rotterdam.
• Neither Gerald nor Peter have a red costume.
• The trapeze artist hears people speaking in Dutch.
• The juggler is performing in Cologne.
• The clown is not wearing a white costume.
• The French audience love the horse riding act.

SUM OF NAILS

Can you make this sum right by moving just 2 nails?

49

MINI-PUZZLE

There are 3 different shapes in this grid. With the help of these shapes, see if you can fill 7 other squares, so that each shape appears just once in each of the rows across and down.

THE CUBE

How many small cubes will the bricklayer need to finish building the big cube?

How many small cubes will there be in the big cube altogether? 24

ON THE ICE!

It has been very cold for many days and now the big lake is completely frozen over. The frozen surface of the lake doubles in size each day. It has taken exactly thirteen days for the lake to become frozen. So, how many days did it take for half the surface of the lake to become frozen?

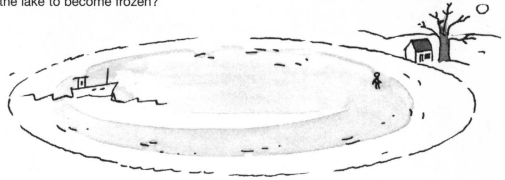

IMPOSSIBLE!

The artist has gone a little crazy! Can you find 7 mistakes in the picture?

WALL OF FIGURES

Each brick in this wall should have a number on it. Each number is the result of multiplying the two numbers on the bricks below. Can you fill in all the numbers?

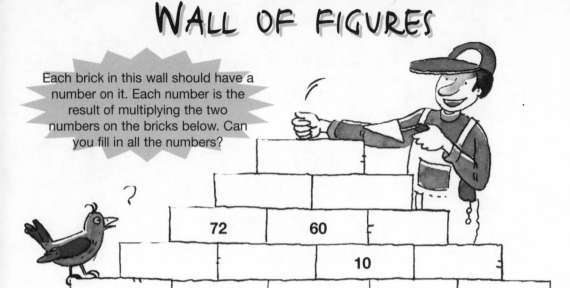

72	60	

| | 10 | |

| 3 | | 3 |

HOOPS AND OVALS

There is a letter where two ovals intersect. Can you replace each letter with one of the numbers from the circles above? Each number can only be used once and the numbers in each oval must add up to 21.

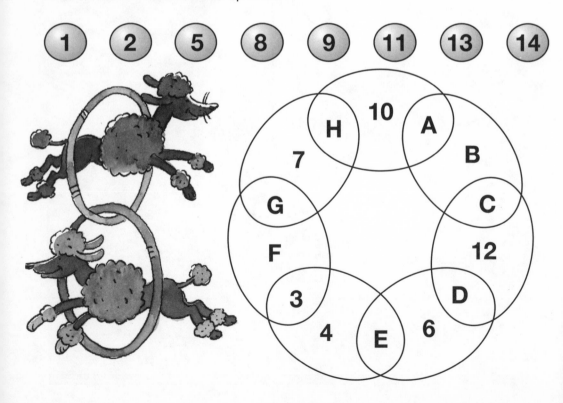

(1) (2) (5) (8) (9) (11) (13) (14)

10   H   A   B
7   C
G   12
F
3   D
4   E   6

JOURNEY BY AIR

There are seats in this aeroplane for 8 passengers. Each seat is numbered. Where does each passenger sit?

- Frances is sitting just behind the pilot. If she wants to look out of the window, she must turn to the left.
- One seat separates the pilot from Catherine.
- Damien is sitting next to Catherine.
- Emma and Kate are sitting side by side.
- Emma is sitting just in front of Bernard.
- Damien does not have a window on his right.
- Damien and Grace are sitting on the same side of the aeroplane, but not one behind the other.
- Alan and Grace are sitting as far away from each other as Frances and Bernard.

Seat 1: ....

Seat 2: Frances .....

Seat 3: ....

Seat 4: ....

Seat 5: ....

Seat 6: ....

Seat 7: ....

Seat 8: ....

SYMBOLS AND NUMBERS

Each symbol represents a different number.
Can you work out what the numbers are?

$$✡ \times ✡ = 100$$
$$✳ + ✳ + ★ = ♣$$
$$★ + ◆ = ♣$$
$$✡ + ✡ + ✡ = ✳ + ✳$$
$$◆ - ✡ = ★$$

♣ =   ★ =   ✡ =   ◆ =   ✳ =

THE ANTIQUE COIN

A coin collector found a coin in a shop which dated from 175 BC. It was a Roman coin and he knew how valuable such a coin could be, especially when it was in such fine condition. Also, the price being asked was very low. But the collector did not buy it. Why not?

WHAT IS IN THE TREE?

Use the parts of words on the leaves to complete the grid. Write in the correct answers and you will find the name of something which is in the tree beneath the arrow.

1. A small cupboard.
2. Blow this up at a party.
3. Lie on this in the garden.
4. Where honey is made!
5. Another word for pills.
6. An insect? Or a game?
7. Places where cars are kept.
8. Not outdoors!

Leaves: ball, loun, gar, hive, ket, cab, tab, cric, ages, inet, in, lets, oon, ger, bee, doors

1
2
3
4
5
6
7
8

SQUARES

How many squares can you count in this big square? Do not be in too much of a hurry to answer '9' ! There are actually a few more!

And how many squares are there below?

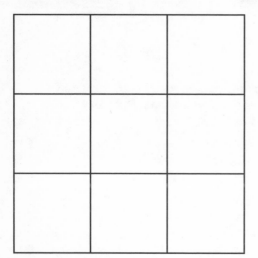

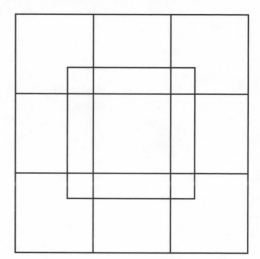

ROMAN FRACTIONS

By moving two nails it is possible to correct this fraction in roman numerals.

You need to move two nails to correct this fraction in roman numerals.

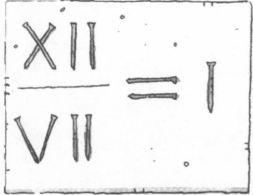

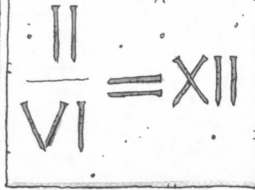

56

THE PERFECT BALANCE

How many turkeys must go on the last see-saw to get a perfect balance. One clue – a gorilla weighs exactly 100 kilos.

A pig weighs ...... kg.
A dog weighs ...... kg.
A sheep weighs ..... kg.
A cat weighs ...... kg.
A turkey weighs ..... kg.

AT THE PICNIC

5 adults and 2 children want to picnic together on a little island in the middle of the river. The problem is they only have one small boat which has room for just one adult or one or two children. The boat is even too small for an adult with a child. So, how can they all get to the island?

AT THE RESTAURANT

Here is the menu for a New York restaurant. The price list (in dollars) is not yet finished. All you know is that a roll cost $1.50.

Can you complete the menu?

- The steak costs as much as a pizza and spaghetti put together.
- 10 rolls cost as much as a portion of chicken.
- The steak is one and a half times more expensive than the chicken.
- The chicken and 2 rolls cost as much as 2 pizzas.
- A fillet of sole and a roll cost as much as a steak and 3 rolls.
- The paella costs half the price of a fillet of sole.

ODD ONE OUT

Underline the odd one out in each row.
Write the first letter of this word
in the circle. What word do you see
reading downward?

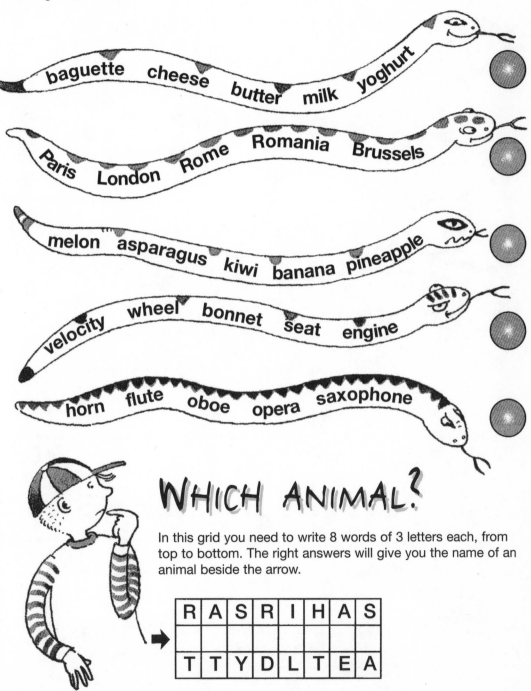

baguette   cheese   butter   milk   yoghurt

Paris   London   Rome   Romania   Brussels

melon   asparagus   kiwi   banana   pineapple

velocity   wheel   bonnet   seat   engine

horn   flute   oboe   opera   saxophone

WHICH ANIMAL?

In this grid you need to write 8 words of 3 letters each, from
top to bottom. The right answers will give you the name of an
animal beside the arrow.

R	A	S	R	I	H	A	S
T	T	Y	D	L	T	E	A

ALL AT SEA!

The 10 battleships above the grid must all find a place in the grid. The ships must not touch. Beside each row, the number shows the amount of squares which can be occupied by a section of a ship in that row. To help you, some squares are already filled.

One tip: write the minus sign (-) in the squares which cannot be filled.

	3	2	3	0	2	3	2	2	3
4					◖				●
1		–		–					
1			■						
5		–		–					
1									
3									●
0									
1		◓							
4								◗	

THE NUMBER CASTLE

Each number on the knight's shields must fit into the castle grid.

1 2 3 4 5 6 7

7 6 5 4 3 2 1

10	73
15	76
18	84
24	86
25	94
31	96
32	99
33	200
40	457
43	704
48	906
53	1016
63	1095

1465	
1908	24889
2131	28531
2137	77743
2772	78073
4751	78938
5327	469283
5384	526042
6458	577937
7935	724903
8420	1587298
	3874608

THE STOLEN VASES

At the police station there is quite a collection of vases from houses which have been burgled. Mrs. Brown has come to find her vase. 'That's my vase!' she says. 'The one which is the most unlike vase number 1.' So, which is Mrs. Brown's vase? How many differences are there between her vase and vase number 1?

SYMBOL SUM

Replace each symbol with a number so that the sum works out correctly. One clue - the numbers 200 and 234 appear in the calculations.

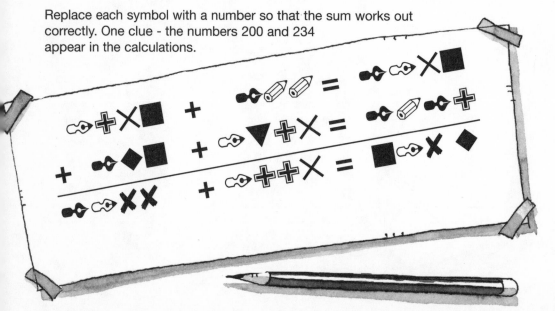

ON YOUR MARKS!

Three runners are ready to start an international cross country run. Mark is from London, Christian is from Amsterdam and Paul is from Paris. Can you tell which runner is which, knowing that:

• Paul is further to the right than Christian.
• The French runner is on the right of Mark.
• Mark is on the right of the Dutch runner.

COMPLETE THE SERIES

Can you complete each row of numbers, following the series?

a. **50 . 53 . 52 . 55 . 54 .   .   .**

b. **4 . 5 . 7 . 11 . 19 . 35 .   .   .**

c. **3 . 6 . 8 . 6 . 12 . 14 . 12 .   .   .**

d. **256 . 128 . 64 . 32 . 16 .   .   .**

FROM 1 - 6

Each fruit in this grid represents a number. The total of the numbers added together is shown to the right and below each column.
Which fruit represents which number?

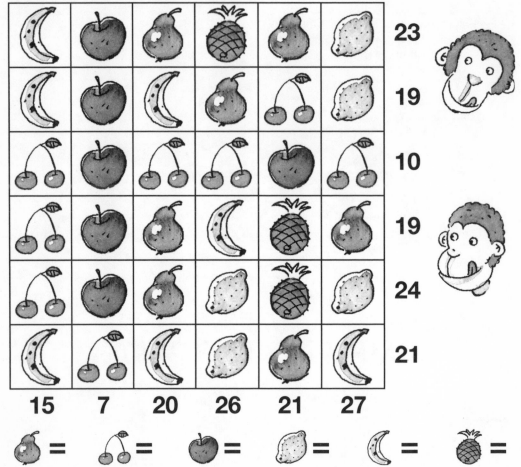

UNDER THE UMBRELLA

All 22 members of the Hip-Hop Club are
sheltering under one umbrella.
They are sticking out on all sides,
yet none of them get wet.
How can this be possible?

THE SECRET CODE

The bank manager has forgotten the secret code number for his safe! He only knows that the code is made up of 4 letters which spell the first name of his best friend. Look at the code grid.
Can you find the secret number for the bank manager?

- A circle indicates the right letter in the wrong place.
- A star indicates the right letter in the right place.

The secret code is:

T	M	A	C	○○☆
E	A	C	M	○○☆
M	C	A	E	○○☆
A	T	R	C	○☆☆

			☆☆☆☆

WEIGHING FOR AND AGAINST

Think and look carefully.
Is this scale really balanced exactly?

THE YELLOW CUBE

This cube is made of red-coloured wood, but the external sides have been painted yellow. Dan must saw through the cube following the black lines.

How many small cubes will he end up with? ....

How many small cubes will be completely red? ....

How many small cubes will have 3 yellow sides? ....

How many small cubes will have 2 yellow sides? ....

How many small cubes will have just 1 yellow side? ....

THE SURGEON

A man and his son were driving along when suddenly their car skidded and collided with an electricity pylon. Sadly, the father was killed instantly. The son was taken to the nearest hospital and taken to the operating theatre. The surgeon came in, pointed to the boy and said, 'I'm sorry, I cannot operate. That boy is my son!' How could this be possible?

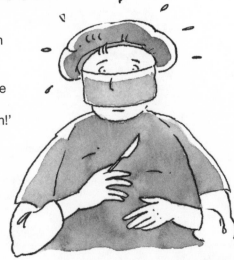

STAMP SWAP-SHOP

2 boys and 2 girls have saved some special edition stamps which they can now swap for toys at a shop.

Which toy does each child choose?
How many stamps must be swapped for each toy?
How old is each child?

	Puzzle	Paints	Book	Car	300 stamps	450 stamps	700 stamps	900 stamps	9 years	10 years	11 years	12 years
Stephen												
Laura												
Christopher												
Valerie												

We know that:
- Laura chooses a book, swapping 500 stamps.
- A 9 year old boy chooses paints.
- The car is chosen by a boy. This is not the most expensive toy.
- The toy costing the most stamps is chosen by the youngest boy.
- Christopher is the oldest child.
- The car is worth more stamps than the puzzle.
- The girl who gives 700 stamps is the oldest of the girls.

NAIL PROBLEM

You only need to move 2 nails to put this sum right.

$$V + V = XX$$

CIRCLE OF NUMBERS

Can you divide the circle into 4 equal parts, so that the numbers in each part will add up to 13?

GHOSTS!

A ghost had been haunting a town. Following a search, three ghosts were brought before the judge, one white, one yellow and one brown. But, as everyone knows, all ghosts look alike, so the only witness could not say which one was guilty.
'No problem!' said the judge. 'I know that a guilty ghost always tells lies, whereas an innocent ghost always speaks the truth.'
The judge could see the white ghost muttering under his breath.
'What did he say?' asked the judge.
'He said that he was the one who haunted the town!' said the yellow ghost.
'You're lying!' said the brown ghost.
'You are not lying!' the judge told the brown ghost.
How did the judge know that the brown ghost was not lying?
Which ghost really was guilty of haunting the town?

A LION MINUS A RAT!

What is the value
of each letter?

$$\begin{array}{r} lion \\ - \ rat \\ \hline 5921 \end{array}$$

$O \times N = 63$

$O \times I = 21$

$O \times L = 42$

$O \times T = 56$

$O \times A = 35$

$O \times R = 28$

THE MYSTERIOUS SENTENCE

If you find the words in this grid, you will discover what happened to Ben on his holidays! The sentence begins in the top left-hand corner, reading from left to right. Above each column are the letters which must be put in the right squares to make the words.

C A A F O	T N O A	R M C	A A P M D	R M Y	G E M R	S A R I I	A S V V C	T H E I	O E N	G O R M	L E
		■									■
		■			■						
				■							
					■			■			■
	■							■	■		

PUZZLE PIECES

Look at the jumbled-up pieces of puzzle underneath the completed picture. There are 3 pieces missing. Which pieces are they?

COLOUR BLOCKS

Each block in the box below must be coloured in, using as few colours as possible.
Blocks of the same colour must not touch.

How many different colours will you need to use?

MAGIC 222

Complete this little grid using the numbers
on the balloons. The sum of the numbers
on each row (across, down and
diagonally) must equal 222.

		73
	74	

ODD ONE OUT

Look carefully at these 6 drawings. One does not belong in the group. Can you say which one it is and why?

There is also an 'odd one out' in this group. Which one is it?

THE SCHOOL PARTY

100 people go to the school party. There are twice as many children as parents, and three times as many parents as teachers. How many children, how many parents and how many teachers are at the party?

AT THE ZOO

Someone has broken the signs showing the names of the animals. Fit the pieces together and you will discover which animals live at this little zoo.

THE RIGHT BALLOON

Look at these 4 balloons. Which one is decorated with no more than 4 stars, less than 3 horizontal lines, exactly 5 vertical lines, less than 2 circles and more than 1 square?

PLAYING CARDS

What is the value of each card symbol (heart, diamond, spade and club)?

74

SUPER SUMS

Finish off these two grids, writing in the numbers or the signs which fit into the empty spaces.

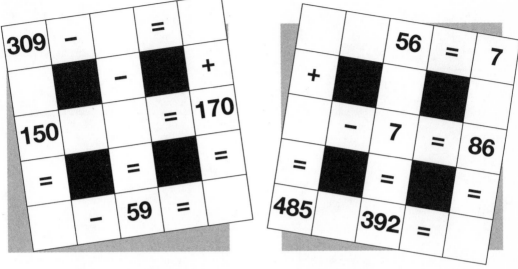

COMBINATIONS

Look at the figures drawn in the white squares. Each one is a combination of two figures shown in the grey squares, one figure in the row across, one figure in the row down. But 7 figures are wrong combinations. Which ones are they?

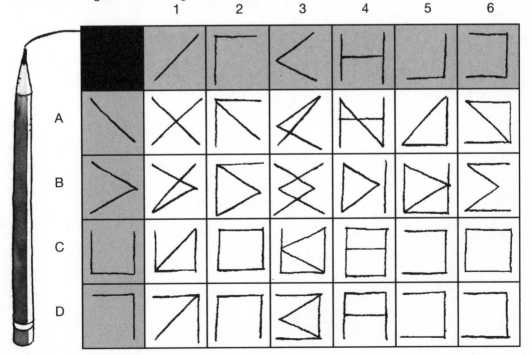

ON THE SCALES

How many bananas must be put on the last set of scales so that they balance?

FIVES AND SEVENS

In this magic grid you need to write the number 5 four times and the number 7 twelve times. To help you, we have already written one 5 and one 7.

The numbers in each row, down, across and diagonally, must add up to 26.

HOLIDAY SOUVENIRS

5 boys are spending their holidays in different countries. Each one wants to bring back a holiday souvenir for his sister.

Find out...
... what is the name of each boy's sister
... which souvenir each boy brings back
... where each boy is spending
his holiday.

Alan

Eric

Emily

Bob

Mary

Gill

Damien

Helen

Danielle

Thomas

We know:
- Danielle does not get a furry kangaroo.
- Alan is bringing back a cowboy hat.
- Gill is getting a Chinese porcelain tea set, but not from Bob.
- It is not Damien who is bringing Emily a statuette of the Little Mermaid from Copenhagen.
- Mary, Tom's sister, does not receive an African mask.
- Eric does not bring back a statuette.
- Helen will not get a hat.
- Damien is not Gill's brother.

Brothers	Sisters	Souvenirs	Continents

THE BRIDGES

On this map we can see a river crossed by 15 bridges. You find yourself near bridge 7 and you want to go to the Information Bureau (i). But as you like crossing bridges, you want to cross each bridge just once. How can you do this?

STARS!

Try putting these 8 stars in the grid so that there is no more than 1 star in each row, across, down and diagonally.

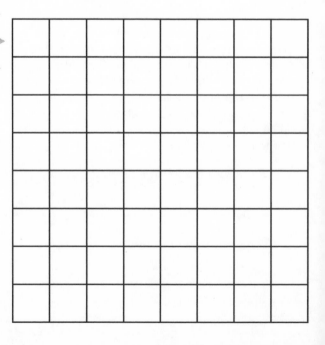

CROSSWORD PUZZLE

Can you see where the jigsaw pieces go to
complete the crossword puzzle?

ANIMAL NOISES

Draw a line to join each animal with the sound it makes

cow	cackles
donkey	grunts
horse	barks
snake	brays
elephant	bellows
hen	croaks
sheep	roars
duck	trumpets
pig	lows
lion	neighs
frog	hisses
dog	quacks
bull	bleats

DOWN THE LANE

In this lane there are 5 houses where 2 boys and 3 girls live. Each of them has a favourite hobby. Write, below each house, the name of the child who lives there and their favourite hobby.

....

....

We can tell you that:
- Catherine's house has more than 3 windows.
- Tim's house has less than 5 windows.
- One of the boys loves skateboarding.
- Catherine's house number is higher than 10.
- A girl who loves ballet dancing lives at number 13.
- Catherine likes swimming.
- The two boys, Tim and Roger, live at numbers 9 and 15.
- Mary does not like dancing.
- One of Tim's neighbours collects stamps.
- Irene lives next to a boy who likes drawing.

BRAINTEASER

When visitors call at Blank Towers, Lord Blank always shows them a large portrait picture in the entrance hall. 'I have no brothers or sisters,' he tells the visitors, 'but the father of the man in the portrait is my father's son.'

Who is the person in the portrait?

OFF WITH HIS HEAD!

'Off with his head!' simply means take away the first letter of each five-letter word to make a four-letter word.

5-letter words

1. To compete unfairly
2. Rather fat
3. Can be eaten at any meal
4. A seat
5. In that place
6. How soldiers often move on foot
7. Decoration on clothes
8. A fruit
9. Seen in the sky, white or grey
10. To drain water from a field

4-letter words

1. Opposite of coldness
2. A shapeless mass of something
3. To understand written words
4. Grows on your head!
5. In this place
6. A curve-topped entrance
7. An attack on something
8. Every
9. Not quiet
10. Makes you scratch!

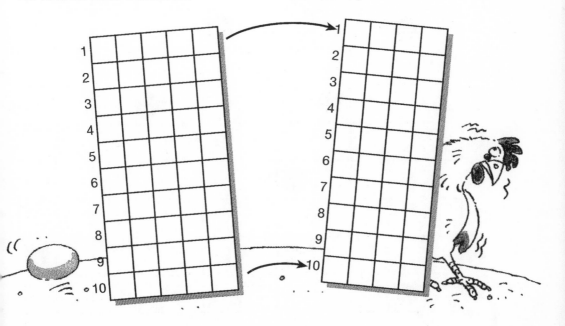

ALL AT SEA!

The 15 battleships shown here above the grid must all find a place in the grid. The ships must not touch. Beside each row, a number shows the amount of squares which can be occupied by a section of a ship in that row.

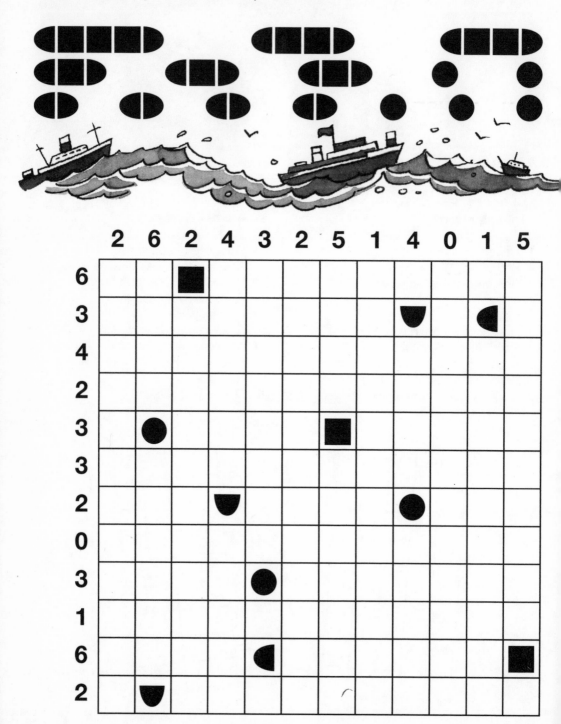

WORD JUMBLE

Here are some words cut into pieces! The letters in each piece have been mixed up. Sort out the letters and join the pieces together to make a word, using the clue to help you.

TAN + LE HPE + = ... (animal)

HC + TALE + OOC = ... (sweet)

CETT +RA + CIH = ... (job)

RAT + KOE + HIC = ... (vegetable)

NIC + LALE + RDE = ... (fairy-tale character)

LAG + ROP + TU = ... country)

MAZE PUZZLE

Find your way through the maze. Each word begins with the last letter of the previous word.

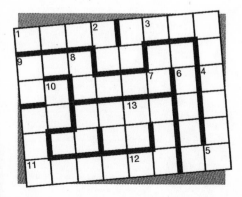

1. Flower
2. Opposite of late
3. Another word for boy
4. Back of the foot
5. Midday meal
6. Grows on your head
7. Flowing water
8. Colour signal for STOP
9. Not wet!
10. This makes dough rise
11. Name of something or someone
12. Joint in your arm
13. These let in the light

THE TWO HALVES

One square can be divided into 2 equal parts in different ways. One possible way is shown in square A. Can you find 5 other ways of dividing squares B, C, D, E and F into 2 equal parts?

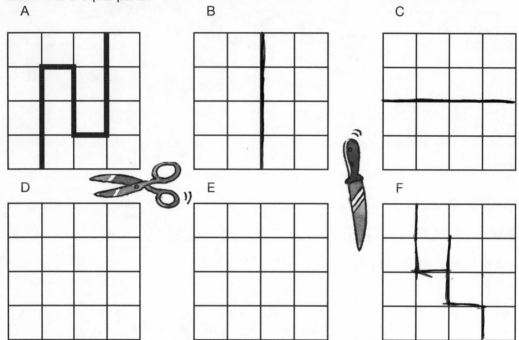

A   B   C

D   E   F

THE MAXICUBE

How many small cubes must be added to complete the big cube?

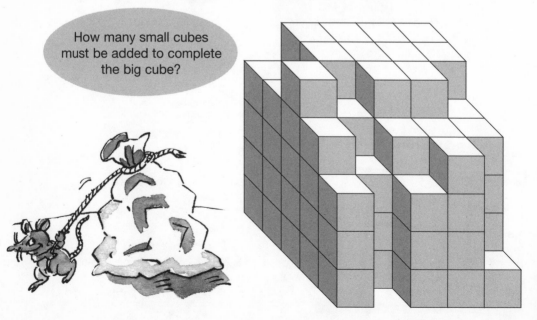

THE FIVE PEN FRIENDS

Annette, Bridget, Carol, Daniel and Errol all write to pen friends who live abroad.
What is the name of each one's pen friend?
How long have they been writing to each other?
How old are each of the foreign pen friends?

	Magali	Kris	Joachim	Sven	Arabel	4 months	6 months	1 year	2 years	4 years	10 years	11 years	12 years	13 years	14 years
Annette															
Bridget															
Carole															
Daniel															
Errol															

We know that:

- Bridget has been writing to Magali for 2 years.
- Errol has been writing to his pen friend, who is a girl, for the longest.
- Annette writes to a boy who is more than 12 years old.
- Carole's pen friend is 11 years old.
- Kenneth has known Daniel for 6 months.
- Bridget's pen friend is older than Annette's pen friend.
- Carole has been writing to her pen friend longer than Daniel.
- Joachim is 11 years old and is not Annette's pen friend.
- Carol started to write 8 months before Annette.
- Sven does not know Daniel.
- Errol's pen friend is 2 years older than Daniel's pen friend.

FLOOR TILES

Each floor tile represents a certain number. The total of the numbers in each row is shown to the right and at the bottom.

THE MEETING

Val is meeting Nicholas. She is waiting on a terrace by the river. Suddenly, almost before Val sees him arrive, Nicholas is there beside her! Val wants to know if he came on foot, by bike or by car. Can you help her find out?

Val knows that:

• Nicholas only uses a back-pack when he rides his bike.
• When it rains, Nicholas travels in a friend's car.
• When Nicholas does not have a back-pack, he does not wear a crash helmet.
• Nicholas is wearing his crash helmet.

SOLUTIONS

The Birds   p.3
From right to left: 3,6,2 11 and 8 birds

Can-Can!   p.3
First row: 22 (+ 2, + 4, + 6, + 8...)
Second row: 15 (+ 5, + 10, + 15, + 20...
Third row: 26 (+ 2, then + 5.)

Male and Female   p.4
ewe & ram; goose & gander:
sow & boar: cow & bull:
doe & buck: nanny & billy

Word Search   p.4

The Seven Differences   p.5

The Sailing Ships   p.6
Ship B (double each number &
3rd arrow different)

Sailors' Knots   p.6
Ropes 1, 2 and 4

Birthday Party!   p.7
1 = Isabel: 2 = Marina: 3: William:
4 = Julie: 5 = Thomas: 6: Mark

Nail Problem!   p.7
I = III - II

Equal Parts   p. 8

Sums in Code   p. 8
631 + 211 = 842
339 + 314 = 653
970 + 525 = 1495

I Spy!   p. 9
1. Nine: 2. Rows 3 & 7: 3. Rows 1 & 5,
rows 3 & 7 4. The black square. 5. The
black triangle. 6. Row 4. 7. No.

Cube Puzzle   p. 10
14 small cubes missing
64 small cubes fit into big cube

Number Cross   p.10
425 − 293 = 132
− ■ − ■ −
393 − 275 = 118
= ■ = ■ =
32 − 18 = 14

Treasure Chest   p.11
December

The Castle Moat   p.11

What Job? Which Pet?   p.12
Christopher: dog and baker
Ralph: pony and teacher

Anne: canary and chauffeur
Juliet: cat and postman

A Cucumber and a Half   **p.12**
Half a cucumber weighs 150 grammes. So, a cucumber and a half weighs 450 grammes

Vehicles   **p.13**
Bus = 1, car = 2, bike = 3, aeroplane = 4, helicopter = 5

On the Farm   **p.13**

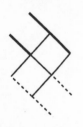

The Matchstick Fish   **p. 14**

Flower Power   **p.15**

3 =   1 =   2 =   5 =   4 =

Dogs' Weigh-In p.15
1 Poodle, 1, Pekingnese, 3 Yorkshire Terriers

The Magic Carpet   **p.16**

Pyramid Puzzle   **p.16**
The young lady's father

Sea Battle   **p.17**

Follow On!   **p.17**
a. 92 and 94 (each time x 2 + 2)
b. 20 and 26 (+ 1, +2, + 3, + 4...)
c. 120 and 720 (x 1, x 2, x 3, x 4...)

The Tree   **p.18**
1. sick; 2. mynah; 3. crumb;
4. tall; 5. May; 6. stool;
7. rattle: 8. feast

Visiting Cards   **p.18**
journalist; architect; translator; musician.

The Matchstick House   **p.19**

The Matchstick Palace   **p.19**

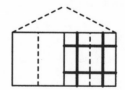

The Clock p.19
It still says 6 o'clock! The time does not change even if you move the hands.

The Holidays p.20
Jeremy: Spain, 1-31 August, staying with an aunt.
Emma: Norway, 20-31 July, hotel
Annette: Luxembourg, 1-15 July, apartment
Tom: Italy, 1-15 August, in tent

The Ship Grid p.21

```
      1 2 3 4
      8 2 9
      7
    4 6
  8 2 0
  1 9 ■ 5 3
6 2 8 ■ ■ 6 5 5
3 5 6 ■ ■ 4 1 6 7 2 3
4 7 8 ■ 3 ■ 2 0 1 ■ ■ 2 7 9
7 8 5 ■ 1 8 9 ■ 1 8 ■ 4 5 4 2 8
3 6 1 ■ 4 9 7 0 ■ 6 0 0 5
```

The Downpour p.21
Mr. Dent is bald!

Fair Shares p.22

Peeling Apples p.22
Giles = 2: David = 3: Ann = 9: Emily = 6: Bruno = 5.

Matchstick Puzzle p.23

Impossible! p.23
Three things did not exist in Ancient Roman times – a radio, a watch and an electricity socket.

The Cube Question p.24
10 cubes are missing

Sheep in the Meadow p.24

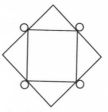

The Storytellers p.25
As Gerald never tells lies, he cannot be in the centre or to the right. So Gerald is to the left, Dennis in the centre and Charles to the right.

Number Grids p.25

```
130 + 198 = 328
 +    ■  -  ■   +
153 - 117 =  36
 =    ■  =  ■   =
283 + 81 = 364
```

```
 9  X 14 = 126
 X    ■  X  ■   +
28  X  3 =  84
 =    ■  =  ■   =
252 - 42 = 210
```

Animal Numbers p.26
cat = 1, owl = 2, dog = 3, pig = 4, cow = 5.

A Series of Letters p.26
1st row: T (jump 2 letters each time)
2nd row: U (jump 1 letter, then 2,3...)

The Bar p.27
John: B & squash, Peter: D and soda, Mark: A & lemonade, Tim: C & water, Luke: E & cherryade

The Twin Clowns p.28
clowns 2 and 7

Twins, or not Twins? p.28
They are two brothers of triplets

An Amazing Apple Tart! p.29
Turn the drawing upside down.

Castle Under Siege p.29

40 10 40
10 [   ] 10
40 10 40

Pyramid of Numbers p.30

181
82 99
34 48 51
13 21 27 24
5   8   13 14 10
2   3   5   8   6   4

The Starry Sky p.30
star = 1, comet = 2, moon = 3, Saturn = 4, space ship = 5

Numbered Furniture p.31
2 x 50 = 100
100 : 5 = 20
(2 x 25) + 50 = 100
2 x 2 x 5 = 20

The Intruder p.31
If the young man really thought he was entering his room, he would not have knocked on the door.

On the See-Saw p.32
5 dogs

Barrier Problem p.32

The Flowers p.33
rose = 25 pesetas; tulip = 17 pesetas; carnation = 21 pesetas. So John paid 193 pesetas.

All at Sea! p.33
yacht = 80, cargo boat = 60, dinghy =

40, submarine = 20

The Tiles p.34
9th tile of 3rd row, 9th tile of 4th row, 4th tile of 5th row, 6th tile of 7th row.

Two Buckets of Water p.34
Fill the 3-litre bucket and empty the water into the 5-litre bucket. Fill the 3-litre bucket again and empty the water into the 5-litre bucket until it is full. This will leave 1 litre in the small bucket. Then empty the 5-litre bucket and pour the 1 litre into the 5-litre bucket. Fill the 3-litre bucket again, and you will have 4 litres in all!

The Unfinished Puzzle p.35
C, E and H

The Letter-boxes p.36

Broken Vase p.36
piece no.6

At the Market p.37
carrots = 30fr. pears = 55fr. bananas = 50fr. grapes = 90fr. potatoes = 10fr.

Newspaper Readers p.37
There were only 3 men. 1 son with his father and grand-father!

Mix-Up! p.38
dance, beans, paste, later, court, nurse, satin, sails, route, limit = nasturtium

Hidden Animals p.38
1. bear; 2. swan; 3. seal;
4. monkey; 5. zebra; 6. camel

Perfect Balance! p.39
3 cones

Enjoy your Meal!   **p. 39**
Claire: spaghetti & squash;
Dawn: roll & water; James: chicken &
lemonade; Matthew: pizza & cola

Stars in a Square   **p.40**
5 1 7 4 8 5 7
4 ☆ 3 ☆ 1 ☆ 4
6 8 2 5 6 2 3
4 ☆ 3 ☆ 8 ☆ 5
1 5 7 1 4 7 1
6 ☆ 2 ☆ 3 ☆ 2
4 3 8 6 5 8 6

The Three Bandits   **p.40**
As George is lying, Gus is not guilty. As
Willy is lying, George is not guilty either.
So only Willy can be guilty.

Pyramid of Eggs   **p.41**

          122
        55   67
      23   32   35
    10   13   19   16
   6   4   9   10   6
  5   1   3   6   4   2

The Twin Grids   **p.41**
Grids 3 and 4

Creepy-Crawlies   **p.42**
spider = 1, beetle = 2, fly = 3, snail = 4,
worm = 5, butterfly = 6

Hens and Eggs   **p.42**
The same – 5 minutes!

The Circles   **p.43**
Circle 7 – the same figures are in each
row, but in a different order.

Star Sum   **p.43**
3517 + 1997 + 3103 + 6791 + 5529 =
20937.

Find the Witness   **p.44**
Room D

The Beehive   **p.45**

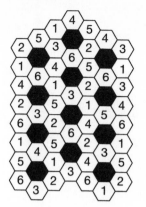

The Hidden Grid   **p.45**

          181
        82   99
      34   48   51
    13   21   27   24
   5   8   13   14   10
  2   3   5   8   6   4

The Magic Square   **p.46**

35	1	6	26	19	24
3	32	7	21	23	25
31	9	2	22	27	20
8	28	33	17	10	15
30	5	34	12	14	16
4	36	29	13	18	11

In a Series   **p.46**
10 (each time x2 and -2).
E and U (jump 3 letters each time)
60 (each time -10, then -5).
V on 32 and N on 2 (alphabet in reverse
and jump a letter each time) and for the
numbers, dividing by two each time).

Coded Letter   **p.47**
Dear Kiwi,
Can you come to see me on Sunday
afternoon for tea? Strange things are
happening in this castle. Suits of
armour walk around, pictures fall from

the walls and I am scared that the castle may be haunted. Please come as soon as you can.
Marguerite Van de Fochy.

Naval Battle p.48

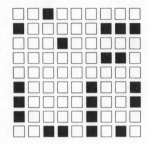

Lift Problem p.48
The lady is not tall enough to reach the lift buttons higher than 8.

Come to the Circus p.49
Gerald: white, juggler,Cologne.
Perry: yellow,clown,Brussels.
William: red,trapeze artist, Rotterdam.
John: blue, horse rider, Paris

Sum of Nails p.49
III + II + I = VI

Mini-Puzzle p.50

The Cube p.50
24 cubes are needed.
There will be 125 small cubes.

On the Ice! p.51
12 days

Impossible! p.51

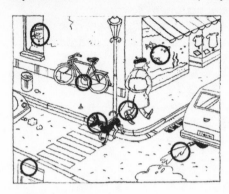

Wall of Numbers! p.52

```
              38880000
          4320      9000
       72        60        150
    12        6        10        15
  4       3       2       5       3
```

Through Hoops and Ovals p.52
A = 2, B = 11, C = 8, D = 1, E = 14, F = 13, G = 5, H - 9

Journey by Air p.53
1 = Alan; 2 = Frances; 3 = Catherine; 4 = Damien; 5 = Emma; 6 = Kate; 7 = Bernard; 8 = Grace

Symbols and Numbers p.54
10 x 10 = 100
15 + 15 + 20 = 50
20 + 30 = 50
10 + 10 + 10 = 15 + 15
30 - 10 = 20

The Ancient Coin p.54
The coin was a forgery. In 175 BC who would have known when Christ would be born?

What is in the Tree? p.55
1. cabinet; 2. balloon; 3. lounger;
4. beehive; 5. tablets; 6. cricket;
7. garages; 8. indoors.
A bluebird is hidden in the tree.

The Squares p.56
14 and 23

Roman Fractions p.56
The two answers are the same:
XII over VI = II

The Perfect Balance p.57
8 turkeys

At the Picnic p.58
First, the two children go across. One of
them stays on the island, whilst the
other goes back. Then, the first adult
travels alone. The child on the island
goes back. Together the two children go
to the island, then one comes back, etc.

At the Restaurant p.58
steak = $22.5, chicken = $15,
sole = $25.5, spaghetti = $13.5
pizza = $9, paella = $12.75

Odd One Out p.59
baguette, (a roll among dairy produce),
Romania, (a country among capital
cities), asparagus (vegetable among
fruit), velocity (speed among parts of a
car), opera (musical work among
instruments)

Which Animal? p.59
antelope

Sea Chase p.60

The Castle of Numbers p.61

The Stolen Vases p.62
vase no.4 (7 differences)

Symbol Sum p.62
1954 + 200 = 2154
234 + 1795 = 2029
2188 + 1995 = 4183

On your Marks! p. 63
15 = Kristian (Holland) 21 =
Mark (Belgium) 8 = Paul (France)

Complete the Series p.63
a. 57 & 56 (each time + 3 then -1)
b. 67 & 131 (+1, +2, +8, +16,
+32, + 64.
C. 24 & 26 (each time x2 then -2).
D. 8 & 4 (each time ÷ 2)

From 1 - 6 p.64
apple = 1,cherry = 2,banana = 3,
pear = 4, pineapple = 5, lemon = 6

Under the Umbrella p.64
It was not raining!

The Secret Code p.65
Marc

Weighing For and Against p.65
Yes!

The Yellow Cube   p.66
He will get 64 cubes; 8 completely red, 8 with three sides yellow, 24 with two sides yellow and 24 with one side yellow

The Surgeon   p.66
The surgeon was the boy's mother

Stamp Swap-Shop   p.67
Stephen: paints, 900, 9 yrs.old
Laura: book, 700, 11 yrs. old.
Christopher: car, 450, 12 yrs.old
Valerie: puzzle, 300, 10 yrs. old

Nail Problem   p.67
X + X = XX

Circle of Numbers   p.68

The Ghost Suspects   p.68
The yellow ghost. The white ghost cannot say that he is guilty (the guilty one always lies, and if the white ghost had been guilty, he would have admitted it.) So now we know that the yellow ghost is lying, he must be the guilty one because he always lies. That means the brown ghost is right and is therefore innocent too.

Lion Minus Rat   p.69
6379 - 458 = 5921

The Mysterious Sentence   p.69
On arriving at my school camp, Mister Ford gave me a camera.

Puzzle Pieces   p.70
2d, 3a and 4c

Colour Blocks   p.71
3 colours

Magic 222   p.71

71	78	73
76	74	72
75	70	77

Odd One Out   p.72
1. Spectacles. The others begin with a 'b'
2. Number 4.

The School Fete   p.72
60 children, 30 parents and 10 teachers

At the Zoo   p.73
giraffe, alligator, crocodile, kangaroo, ostrich, monkey

The Right Balloon   p.74
balloon number 3

Playing Cards   p.74
heart = 5, spade = 3, club = 2, diamond = 0

Super Sums   p.75

$309 - 79 = 230$
$+ \blacksquare - \blacksquare +$
$150 + 20 = 170$
$= \blacksquare = \blacksquare =$
$459 - 59 = 400$

$392 : 56 = 7$
$+ \blacksquare \times \blacksquare +$
$93 - 7 = 86$
$= \blacksquare = \blacksquare =$
$485 - 392 = 93$

Combinations   p.75
3A, 5A, 4B, 6B, 4C, 5C, 3D

On the Scales   p.76
4 bananas

Fives and Sevens   p.76
7 7 5 7
7 5 7 7
7 7 7 5
5 7 7 7

Holiday Souvenirs   p.77
Alan: Danielle, hat, America
Damien: Helen, mask, Africa
Bob: Emily, statuette, Germany
Eric: Gill, tea set, China
Thomas: Mary, kangaroo, Australia

The Bridges   p.78
In the right order – 7, 8, 9, 11, 10,
6, 5, 4, 2, 3, 15, 14, 12, 13 and 1.
(There are some other ways.)

Such Stars!   p.78

There are some other possibilities.

Crossword Puzzle   p.79

L ■ W E T
A W A Y ■
M E T E R
P ■ E ■ ■
S T R I P

Cries of Animals   p.79
cow lows; donkey brays; horse
neighs; snake hisses; elephant
trumpets; hen cackles; sheep
bleats; duck quacks; pig grunts;
lion roars; frog croaks; dog
barks; bull bellows

Down the Lane   p. 80
no.7: Mary collects stamps
no.9: Tim likes skateboarding
no.11: Catherine goes swimming
no.13: Irene likes dancing
no.15: Roger likes drawing

Brainteaser   p.80
Lord Blank

Chop off the Head   p.81
cheat, heat; plump, lump;
bread, read; chair, hair;
there, here; march, arch;
braid, raid; peach, each;
cloud, loud; ditch, itch

On the Sea   p.82

Word Jumble   p.83
elephant; chocolate; architect;
artichoke; Cinderella; Portugal

Maze Puzzle   p.83
1. rose; 2. early; 3. youth;
4. heel; 5. lunch; 6. hair;
7. river; 8. red; 9. dry;
10. yeast; 11. title 12. elbow;
13. windows

The Two Halves   p.84

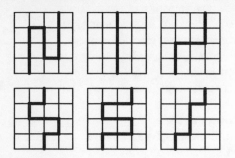

The Maxicube   p.84
24 cubes

The Five Penfriends   p.85
Annette; Sven, 4 months, 13 yrs.
Bridget; Magali, 2 years, 14 yrs.
Carole; Joachim, 1 year, 11 yrs.
Daniel; Kenneth, 6 months, 10 yrs.
Errol; Arabel, 4 years, 12 yrs.

Floor Tiles   p.86

-3   -6   -1   -2   -5   -4

The Meeting   p.86
Nicky wears a helmet, so he also
wears his back-pack. He has come
by bicycle.